PRAYERS
FOR
ALL OCCASIONS

Our God is one God in Three Persons. All our prayers are offered to the Blessed Trinity— usually to the Father, through the Son, in the Holy Spirit.

PRAYERS
FOR
ALL OCCASIONS

Edited by
Rev. Francis Evans

Illustrated

CATHOLIC BOOK PUBLISHING CO.
New York

NIHIL OBSTAT: Daniel V. Flynn, J.C.D.
Censor Librorum

IMPRIMATUR: Patrick J. Sheridan
Vicar General, Archdiocese Of New York

(T-917)

3 4 5 6 7 8 9 10 11 12 13 14 15

CONTENTS

Foreword

Today many Catholics are seeking ways to pray. They are convinced more than ever that they need to pray. They know that, as the Second Vatican Council has stated, "the spiritual life is not limited solely to participation in the Liturgy. Christians are indeed called to pray with their brothers and sisters, but they must also enter into their room to pray to the Father in secret."

There are innumerable ways in which to pray and many methods of prayer. One of the greatest helps to prayer for most people is a book of prayers. It puts at our fingertips a precious treasury of words by which we can approach God every day. Such ready-made prayers imprint on our minds the sentiments that the Church wants us to have in prayer.

Prayers of this type also convey a deeper knowledge and understanding of the Church's teaching. In a subtle and unobtrusive fashion they teach the faith while allowing us to approach God. By using them we not only get closer to God but also get to know Him better with every passing day.

It goes without saying that we can also pray in our words instead of words found on a printed page—and indeed we must do so. However, ready-made prayers are there for those times when we do not know what to say and need help in speaking to God. We need the help of past ages as well as present trends to say what we feel and what we should feel.

This new prayerbook is presented as one such aid. It combines the best features of both traditional and contemporary prayers. It presents timely prayers, prayers that fit neatly into every phase of our daily lives. It gives all of us reasons for praying in every state of life, every state of mind, in times of sorrow, in times of joy, and in times of holiday as well.

Every effort has been made to insure that this book will be easy to use and attractive to the person praying. The text is printed in large pleasing typeface and in red and black. The inspiring colorful illustrations will help keep our minds on Jesus and through Him on the other Persons of the Blessed Trinity.

May all who use this prayerbook achieve a deeper and more vital spiritual life. May it lead them ever closer to the eternal union with the living God.

PRAYER IS CONDUCIVE TO EVERY STATE IN LIFE—No one has a premium on prayer. Whatever our state in life, we must cultivate a solid prayer life, a true dialoguing with God. In this connection, any event or any state will provide reasons of its own for this dialogue.

PRAYERS FOR DIFFERENT STATES OF LIFE

Christians are called to pray always, as we have already seen. This is not an easy thing to do, especially in our hectic times. Hence, over the years many reasons for prayer have evolved and become part of a time-honored mechanics of prayer. This section makes use of the specific states of people's lives as the starting point for praying. The rationale for each prayer is simply a person's membership in a state of life.

What this actually does is take account of the person's life situation in formulating a prayer life for him/her. Previously, we were asked to pray at morning, midday, and evening—and that is all well and good. However, it was possible to lose sight of these moments in the press of the problems of our daily activities. This section, based on that very life itself, is an apt reminder that our prayer life is not relegated to moments but to our very life. It must continue with our everyday life— no matter what our task.

Indirectly, then, this type of praying has a closer relation to us, affords us a *more cogent reason for praying, and reminds us of our ultimate goal even while we are pursuing our everyday goals in life. It gets us in the habit of praying at any time in our daily schedule.*

The prayer formulas in this section are not necessarily exclusive. They may be used by persons who are not part of a particular state in life (used in the broad sense) to pray for those who are—for example, religious. This can easily be done by "converting" the prayers through the simple substitution of the pronouns—thus giving us a ready-made set of prayers for common states of life.

Prayer of the Aging

May Christ keep me ever young
"to the greater glory of God."
For old age comes from Him,
old age leads to Him,
and old age will touch me
only insofar as He wills.
To be "young" means to be hopeful,
energetic, smiling—and clear-sighted.
May I accept death in whatever guise
it may come to me in Christ,

that is, within the process of the development of life.

A smile (inward and outward) means facing
with mildness and gentleness
whatever befalls me.

Jesus, grant me to serve You,
to proclaim You,
to glorify You,
and to manifest You,
to the very end through all the time
that remains to me of life,
and above all through my death.

Lord Jesus,
I commit to Your care my last years,
and my death;
do not let them impair or spoil
the work I have so dreamed of achieving
for You.

Prayer of Altar Boys

Dear Lord Jesus,
thank You for calling me
to serve You at Your holy altar
during the celebration of the Eucharist.
I know that the priest takes Your place
when, together with Your people
and in the name of the Church,

he makes present again
Your Passion, Death, and Resurrection.

Help me to carry out my role
in this memorial of the Last Supper
with dignity and precision
and with full interior participation.
Let me so remain united with You on earth
that I may one day share Your glory in
  heaven.

Prayer of Business Persons

Lord Jesus,
I am a business person,
engaged in commercial enterprises.
I have to work hard to earn my salary
and I do not always remember
to put my Christianity to work in the mar-
  ket-place.
Please forgive me for this,
and help me in the future
to keep the public interest ever in mind.

I know I cannot change the world by myself,
but I can try in my own little way
to be more honest,
more truthful and more trustworthy
in my business life.
Help me, Lord,
for I cannot do it without You.

Prayer of Extraordinary Ministers
of Communion

Lord God,
I thank You for calling me
to serve You and Your people in this community
as an extraordinary minister of the
  Eucharist.
You know that I could never be worthy
of such an exalted honor.
Help me to be less unworthy
by remaining free from sin.

Let me nourish Your people
with the witness of my life
as I feed them with the Body of Christ.
Grant Your strength and holiness
to all Your extraordinary ministers
and make them worthy to bring Christ to
  others.

Prayer of Farmers

Lord God,
King of the Universe,
You are the sole source
of growth and abundance.
With Your help I plant my crops
and by Your power they give forth a harvest.

Grant me the grace always to work
with all my strength and ingenuity
in cultivating the soil
so that it will bring forth fruits
for my benefit
and the benefit of all who will use them.

Make me ever aware that without my part
in the work of harnessing the goods of the
    earth
these particular goods would be lacking
to my brothers and sisters in this world.
Enable me at the same time to realize
that without Your part in this process
I would be working in vain.
Accept my thanks for Your continuous
    past help
and Your never-failing assistance in the fu-
    ture.

Prayer of Fathers

Heavenly Father,
You have been pleased to let me be called
by the name that is Yours from all eternity.
Help me to be worthy of that name.
May I always be for my children a source of
    life—
corporal, intellectual, and spiritual.

Enable me to contribute in great part
to their physical growth by my work,
to their mental advancement by good
  schooling
and to their supernatural life by my prayer
  and example,
so that they may become complete human
  beings
and true children of their heavenly Father.

Let me be conscious that my actions
are far more important than my words.
May I always give my children a good example
in all the situations of life.
May I wear my successes modestly,
and may my failures find me undaunted;
may I be temperate in time of joy
and steadfast in time of sorrow.
May I remain humble after doing good
and contrite after doing evil.
Above all, may I scrupulously respect
my children's rights as human persons
and their freedom to follow a rightly-
  formed conscience,
while at the same time fulfilling my duty to
  guide them
in the way given us by Your Son Jesus.

Prayer of Fiances

O Lord,
we thank You for this wonderful gift of our
    love
which You have generously granted us
and which allows us to build
a true communion of persons between us—
provided we remain ever open to You,
the source of all love.
Help us to continue to love each other
and accept each other as we are, uncondi-
    tionally,
as we get to know each other better.
Make us generous in giving
and humble in receiving.

Enable us to communicate to one another
all our joys, sufferings, and desires
and all our hopes, sorrows, and difficulties.
Give us the power of Your love
that we may forget self and live for each
    other
so that we may have truly one spirit,
in preparation for the time
when You will send us children
to add to our union and love.

Prayer of Grandparents

O Lord,
I know that every period of our lives

has its responsibilities as well as its joys.
Today, it seems that grandparents have
either too little use
or too much—
either we are shunted aside to do nothing
or we are called upon to do everything.
Help me to know just where my duties lie
in my particular situation
and carry them out as best I can.
Take care of my family—
my children and their children.
Inspire them all to follow Your Son
and lead truly Christian lives.
Keep all of us in Your loving care,
never let us turn away from You,
and help us in the end to receive the joy
of entering into Your glorious presence for-
    ever.

Prayer of Homemakers

Dear Lord,
in the minds of most people
making a home is a job of little import
and even less talent.
Help me to realize that the opposite is the
    case—
it is the most important job of all
and it requires a multitude of talents.
Providing a home for living persons

who are made in Your image
means helping them inevitably get closer to
  You.
By my slight efforts
I can influence the members of my family
in hundreds of ways
to become better people and better Christians.

Grant me the grace to know how to handle
  any situation,
the strength to do the ordinary everyday
  things,
the love to overcome all animosities,
and the joy to dispel all boredom.
Help me to grow as a person every day,
to fulfill myself in all the areas
that are necessary for a homemaker—
loving relationships, mental effort, manual
  work.
Give me the strength to bring my family
  closer to Jesus
not so much by my words as by my actions.

Prayer of Laborers

Lord God,
I know that all labor likens us to You—
we continue Your work of creation.
Without manual labor
the world would ultimately grind to a halt.

So I know that my job is important.
But even more my job is important in form-
   ing me
and making me a better person and Christian.
It enables me to give myself to others;
it forces me to be less selfish
and gives me a different outlook on life.
It makes me see that all human beings are
   in this life together
and must work together to get ahead.

Thank You for making it possible for us
to work and to grow.
Grant me the strength to keep working
and to earn a decent wage to take care of
   my family.
Let me give an honest day's work for a
   day's pay
and keep me faithful to You every day of
   my life.

Prayer of Lay People

O Lord,
help me to exercise my lay apostolate
where I work or practice my profession,
or study or reside,
or spend any leisure time
or have my companionships.

Grant that I may become the light of the world
by conforming my life to my faith.
By practicing honesty in all my dealings,
may I attract all whom I meet
to the love of the true and the good,
and ultimately to the Church and to Christ.

Inspire me to share in the living conditions
as well as the labors, sorrows, and aspirations
of my brothers and sisters,
thus preparing their hearts
for the worship of Your saving grace.
Enable me to perform
my domestic, social, and professional duties
with such Christian generosity
that my way of acting will penetrate
the world of life and labor.

Teach me to cooperate
with all men and women of goodwill
in promoting whatever is true,
whatever is just,
whatever is holy, and whatever is lovable.
Let me complement the testimony of life
with the testimony of the Word,
so that I will proclaim Christ

to those brothers and sisters
who can hear the Gospel
through no one else except me.

Prayer of Law Enforcers

Lord God,
You have created a marvelous world
which is permeated by a wondrous sense of
    order.
Yet human beings have a tendency
to war against order on their level.
That is the reason why there are people like
    me
who work at maintaining order in society.

Help me to use my authority with under-
    standing and restraint
and without bias or anger.
Let me remember that in carrying out my
    function
I am sharing in Your Divine Providence in
    the universe
so that the people in this world can live full
    lives
and grow in the knowledge and love of
    You,
of Your Son, and of the Holy Spirit.

Prayer of Leaders of Song

Dear Jesus,
thank You for endowing me with a pleasant voice
and for calling me to use it in Your liturgical rites.
Let me never be puffed up by my singing in church
but ever give the credit to Your gift.

Help me to lead the singing in such a way
that others will be brought to fuller participation
in the celebration of the Eucharist.
Keep me aware that by helping to celebrate
Your Paschal Mystery,
I am helping to bring Your redemption to the world
and the world to You in return.

Prayer of Lectors

Dear Jesus,
thank You for calling me to be a lector
at Your Eucharistic celebrations.
Let me take this role seriously
and diligently prepare myself for it
by studying the sacred texts before Mass
and by striving to be a better Christian.

By my physical action of reading,
I am the instrument through whom You
  become present
to the assembly in Your Word
and through whom You impart Your
  teachings.
Let nothing in my manner disturb Your
  people
or close their hearts to the action of Your
  Spirit.
Cleanse my heart and my mind
and open my lips that I may worthily proclaim Your Word.

Prayer of Members of the Armed Forces

O Lord,
you are the God of hosts.
Strengthen us who are members
of our country's armed forces.
Make us prepare so well to defend our
  country
that we will eliminate the need to do so.
In serving our country
may we be rendering service to You.

Make us loyal to our loved ones
in spite of separations of every kind.
Keep us devoted to Your Church
in spite of the pressures of our duties.

Help us to lead others to You
by the example we give to our comrades-in-
arms.

Prayer of Mothers

Father in heaven,
grant me the grace to appreciate the dignity
which You have conferred on me.
Let me realize that not even the Angels
have been blessed with such a privilege—
to share in Your creative miracle
and bring new Saints to heaven.

Make me a good mother to all my children
after the example of Mary,
the Mother of Your Son.
Through the intercession of Jesus and
Mary
I ask Your continued blessings on my family.
Let us all be dedicated to Your service on
earth
and attain the eternal happiness of Your
Kingdom in heaven.

Prayer of Parents for Children

Lord God,
we want to be true cooperators in grace

and witnesses of faith
for our children.
We know that we have a duty
to educate them in the faith
by word and example.
We also know that we must help them
in choosing a vocation,
carefully promoting any religious vocation
that they may have.

Help us to carry out this sacred trust
all the days of our lives.
Teach us how to dialogue with our children
and share the special benefits
that each generation can offer one another.
Enable us to stimulate them
to take part in the apostolate
by offering them good example,
effective advice, and willing assistance.
May we learn from them how to be open to
    life
and remain ever young in faith, hope, and
    love.

Prayer of Parish Committee Members

O Lord,
You have made me a part of the parish
    committee

whose members have been brought together by the communion
created by Your Word and the Eucharist.
Let me strive to insure that our committee
will be a true forum of opinion
that will act from a consensus
rather than a plurality or majority of votes.
I am called to represent my co-parishioners
and to be a spokesperson for the community.

Help me to speak truly in the people's
name
and express their convictions, ideas, and
visions.
As a co-worker with the parish team of
ministers,
may I never merely endorse the decisions
of that team,
but weigh them carefully and give my honest opinion—
without fear, rancor, or prejudice.
Lastly, let me look beyond parish interests
and consider diocesan and universal ones
as well as civic, national, and human af-
fairs.

Prayer of Pregnant Women

Lord God,
Creator of all things,

You have been pleased to enable my hus-
    band and me
to collaborate with You in conceiving a
    child.
Thank You for Your gracious gift.
Help me to guard this new life carefully
and do nothing to hurt it in any way.

After my child's birth, let me lavish him/
    her with love
and bring him/her up in Your love and ser-
    vice,
so that he/she will become a child of Yours
and inherit Your Kingdom.
Be with me, O Lord, in this greatest of
    tasks
to comfort, strengthen, calm, and en-
    lighten me.

Prayer of Priests

Dear Jesus,
despite my unworthiness
and through the impulse of Your goodness
You have been pleased to raise me to the
    dignity
of the holy priesthood.
You made me not only Your minister

but the voice of Your sublime wisdom as well

and the dispenser of Your mysteries.

I am filled with joy, love, and gratitude to You

for this singular privilege that I have received,

and I am saddened by my failures to respond as I ought

to Your great generosity.

Grant Your light to my mind

that I may daily dispense in greater abundance

the fruits of Your redemption of all human beings.

Help me to be a genuine *pontifex,* a bridge-builder,

between You and Your people,

and enable me to be truly "another Christ" in the world.

Prayer of Professional People

O Lord,

I am what is known as a member of a profession—

that is, one which required special training as well as long years of study.

Most of all, it demanded a talent for understanding
that is Your gift to me.
Let me realize that such talent is given
for the good of the whole human race,
not to enrich myself with an overabun-
   dance
of the goods of this world.

Grant that I may never abuse my office
nor that knowledge that has been given
   me.
May I instead so utilize my talents
that others may see in me
the reflection of Your infinite perfections.
Then may they be drawn to the surpassing
   knowledge
of You and Your beloved Son
in the unity of the Holy Spirit.

Prayer of Religious

Lord Jesus,
I thank You with all my heart
for the privilege of serving You in the religious life.
Let me be convinced that this is the ideal
   way
in which I can live life to the full.
By taking the vow of poverty,
I did not so much give up all things;

rather I have gained the power to use all
    things
in Your service.
By taking the vow of chastity
I did not so much give up my sexual side
or the ability to love;
rather I am enabled to love You without
    limit
and all people in You.
By taking the vow of obedience,
binding myself to the will of legitimate au-
    thority,
I did not so much give up my own fulfill-
    ment;
rather I became free to use my God-given
    gifts
in ways that ensure my truest self-fulfill-
    ment.
In summoning me to be truly Christian,
You have called me to be truly human
and totally involved in building Your King-
    dom on earth.

Prayer of Scholars and Researchers

Lord God,
as we give ourselves to the study
of the various intellectual disciplines
and cultivate the arts,
make us realize that we can do very much

to elevate the human family
to a more sublime understanding
of truth, goodness, and beauty
and to the formation of considered opin-
ions
that will have universal value.
Thus, humankind will be more clearly en-
lightened
by that marvelous Wisdom
which was in Your presence for all eternity.

Grant that we may be less subjected to material things
and so be drawn more easily
to the worship and contemplation of You,
our Creator.
By the impulse of Your grace
make us disposed to acknowledge the
Word of God,
Who before becoming flesh—
in order to save all and sum up all in Himself—
was already in the world
as the true Light that enlightens every person.

Prayer of Shut-Ins

Dear Lord,
because of my difficulty in getting around
I am no longer able to go wherever I please

and am at the mercy of others to be taken
out of this house.
Let me not withdraw from the outside
world
but continue to be interested in it.
For You are there as well as here with me;
You are everywhere in this magnificent
world You made.

Enable me to realize that all the different
stages of life
are a gift from You;
and each age has its own rewards
as well as its problems.
Let me thank You for each new day's life
and use that day to grow in grace
and in the knowledge and love of You.
Help me when I am tired
and grant me the strength to go on.
And at the end of my journey through life
let me see Your glory in heaven.

Prayer of Single People

O Lord,
after much prayer and reflection
it is my belief
that I can best serve You in the single state.
Let me be true to my vocation to this life
and never do anything to sully it.

As I freely give up the benefits of married
   life,
I am aware that I also give up its difficulties
and receive in turn the benefits of the single
   state.
Enable me to appreciate the freedom at my
   disposal
from cares and concerns of spouses and
   children,
from a highly structured life-style,
and from the legitimate demands of family
   members.
Help me to make good use
of the added time I have available.
Inspire me to give of myself to others,
to be an example to my married friends
and a comfort to my single friends.
May I ever realize that whether single or
   married
our one concern should be to serve You
   each day
and to serve others for Your sake.
Grant that I may be so attached to You
that I may never feel lonely in my chosen
   state.

Prayer of Spouses

Lord,
bless this dear person

whom You have chosen to be my spouse.
Make his/her life long and blessed.
May I become a great blessing to him/her,
a sharer in all his/her sufferings and sor-
    rows,
and a suitable helper in all his/her changes
    and vagaries in this life.
Make me lovable forever in his/her eyes
and forever dear to him/her.
Keep me from all unreasonableness of pas-
    sion and humor.
Make me humble and giving,
strong, dedicated, appreciative, prudent,
    and understanding.
May we ever take delight in each other,
according to Your blessed Word,
both sharing in Your Divine love.

Prayer of Students

God of Light and Wisdom,
thank You for giving me
a mind that can know
and a heart that can love.
Help me to keep learning every day—
no matter what the subject may be.
All knowledge leads to You;
let me know how to find You and love You
in all the things You have made.

Encourage me when the studies are hard
and when I am tempted to give up.

Enlighten me when my brain is slow
and let me to grasp the truth held out to me.
Enable me to put my knowledge to use
in building the Kingdom of God on earth
so that I may enter the Kingdom of God in
heaven.

Prayer of Teachers

Lord Jesus Christ,
imbue me with the knowledge
of both secular and religious subjects
that is necessary to my task on earth.
Let me have the suitable qualifications
and a pedagogical skill
that is in harmony with the discoveries
of the contemporary world.
Help me to be united with my students
by the bond of love,
and work in partnership with their parents
to stimulate the students to act for themselves.
Even after their graduation
let me continue to assist them
with advice and friendship.

Bestow on me an apostolic spirit
to bear witness,
both by life and by instruction,
to the unique Teacher—
You, Jesus Christ.

Prayer of Travelers

Lord God,
I am presently embarked on a journey
in pursuit of some good.
Grant that I may travel in safety,
without undue disturbance or worry,
and ultimately attain the goal I seek.

Let me also keep in mind
that I am on another and more important
    journey—
through life.
Keep me ever safe and close to You
as I travel the sometimes hazardous road
toward Your Kingdom in heaven.

Enable me to follow the guidelines
given us by Your Son Jesus
so that I may arrive safely at my eternal
    destination
with You in heaven.

Prayer of the Unemployed

Dear Lord Jesus Christ,
You wanted all who are weary
to come to You for support.
Lord, I am worn out
by my inability to find wage-earning work.
Day after day, my worry and fear grows
as the rejections of my applications mount.

I am able and willing to work—
but I cannot find a worthwhile job.
Please help me to obtain one soon
so that I can support myself and my family
in a decent way.
If it is Your will that I wait longer,
enable me to worry less
and to take advantage of the time available
to get closer to You.
Let me realize that there are other ways
to bring about Your Kingdom on earth
besides salaried work.
Help me to make use of them
so that I may continue to grow as a person
for Your greater glory.

Prayer of Widows and Widowers

Lord Jesus Christ,
during Your earthly life You showed com-
    passion
on those who had lost a loved one.
Turn Your compassionate eyes on me
in my sorrow over the loss of my life's part-
    ner.
Take him/her into Your heavenly Kingdom
as a reward for his/her earthly service.
Help me to cope with my loss
by relying on You even more than before.

Teach me to adapt to the new conditions of
    my life
and to continue doing Your will as I see it.
Enable me to avoid withdrawing from life
and help me give myself to others,
so that I may continue to live in Your grace
and to do the task that You have laid out
    for me.

Prayer of Workers

O Lord, our Creator,
You imposed a duty on all human beings
to work together to build up the world.
Help us to develop the earth
by the work of our hands
and with the aid of technology
in order that it may bear fruit
and become a dwelling worthy of the whole
    human family.

When we do this
or consciously take part in the life of social
    groups,
we are carrying out Your plan
manifested at the beginning of time
that we should subdue the earth,
perfect creation,
and develop ourselves.
Let us realize that

we are also obeying Christ's command
to place ourselves at the service of others
in bringing forth a more human world,
through Your Son Jesus Christ
in the unity of the Holy Spirit.

Prayer of the Young

Lord Jesus,
You always showed great love for the
    young
and the Gospels are filled with incidents
    about the young—
children in general and the centurion's son,
the rich young man and Jairus' daughter.

Please pour down Your grace to help me
in my growing and formative years.
Enable me to take advantage of all the
    good things
while avoiding the many pitfalls
of this age.

Grant that I may follow the example of
    youthful Saints
in remaining devoted to You.
At the same time, let me grow into the
    adult
that You want me to be,
so that I may carry out my vocation in life
for the good of myself and others
as well as for Your honor and glory.

PRAY ALWAYS—IN ANY STATE OF MIND— States of mind provide opportunities for prayer that are ever fresh. Learning to pray in accord with our states of mind will give us an inexhaustible source for prayers and help us stay united to God.

PRAYERS FOR DIFFERENT STATES OF MIND

A *state of mind is something that is always with us as we go through life. At every moment we are in one state of mind or other by the simple nature of being human. This section is intended to show how we can pray in accord with the particular state of mind that may be ours at any given time.*

Naturally, the more negative states of mind lend themselves more easily to prayer—for we know that we need help to get out of them. The value of such prayer is that it places us in contact with our God and pulls us out of ourselves—even if only for a few moments. At the same time, it obtains aid for us in a particular and difficult time of our daily schedule. Finally, it sometimes dissipates the negative state of mind at once.

Positive states of mind are also represented in the prayers given below—times of gratitude, joy, mystical insight, serenity, and success. The value of such prayer is that it prevents us from forgetting God when things are going well and reminds us that all we have is only important insofar as God is part of the picture. It keeps us ever aware of our ultimate goal.

Needless to say, many other states of mind could have been represented by the prayers. The ones included herein have been chosen because of their more or less universal appeal. They can act as fitting models for the composition of prayers for other states and they can get us in the habit of praying in any state of mind throughout our lives.

Prayer in Time of Anger

Lord Jesus,
there is anger in my heart
and I cannot root it out.
I know that I should calm down
and offer the hurt and disappointment to
    You
but my emotion is running away with me.
Help me to overcome this weakness
and give me peace of heart as well as mind.
Let me learn from this experience
and grow into a better human being.

Prayer in a Bad Mood

Heavenly Father,
I awoke this morning in a bad mood
and I have been unable to shake it so far.

Everything bothers me
and everyone rubs me the wrong way.
I just cannot seem to get my true bearings.
Help me to think of Your salvation—
Your countless gifts and overwhelming
   love for me.

Let me relax and forget life's cares
by placing myself wholly in Your hands.
Grant that this mood will soon pass
and I will be able to bask in Your love
and communicate it to others.

Prayer in Time of Change

Eternal and ever-living God,
I am involved in a major change in my life
and it is quite unsettling.
I know that for us creatures
change is an indication of life,
but I still find it hard to accept.

Enable me to see Your hand in it,
subtly bringing about Your plan for me
and enabling me to come closer to You.
Make me appreciate the many good aspects of change
and learn to live with the bad aspects.
Teach me to be pliable and adaptable to
   any change,
fully aware that once change stops for me
I will no longer be alive on this earth.

Prayer in Time of Controversy

Lord Jesus Christ,
I am involved in a bitter controversy
in which it is very difficult to tell who is
    right and who is wrong.
I cannot understand why these things take
    place
among people who are trying to live Chris-
    tian lives,
and I wish I were not involved in it.

Let me realize that controversy is a fact of
    life
and that even Your life was filled with it.
Help me to accept whatever comes in a
    spirit of resignation
and teach me to be better from this experi-
    ence.
Grant that I may resolve the controversy
in a Christian manner
and lead others to You because of it.

Prayer in Time of Criticism

Lord God,
I am the butt of severe criticism
on the part of others
and I do not know how to react to it.
Help me to know what to do
and to carry it out without fear or hesita-
    tion.

Let me fear nothing except to be faithless to
You
while avoiding bitterness, defensiveness, or
retaliation.

Grant that I may have the moral strength
to keep my poise and my faith in myself
because they are founded on You.
If I deserve the criticism, let me realize it
so that I may change my ways.
If I do not deserve it,
let me be gracious in being vindicated,
in imitation of Your Son, our Lord Jesus
Christ.

Prayer in Time of Decision

Lord God, King of heaven and earth,
I am facing a difficult decision in my life
and I do not know what road to take.
You have given me the awesome power to
choose freely
as well as the intelligence to choose wisely.
Inspire me to make the right decision
no matter what it may be.

Let me carefully weigh the reasons on all
sides
from a human point of view
and then rely on Your grace for Divine
help.

When the decision has been reached,
let me not look back,
in the firm knowledge that I have done my
part
and have made a right decision in Your
eyes.

Prayer in Time of Despair

Lord God,
I know I am close to despair.
I feel so tempted to give up,
to withdraw from life and religion
and let the world simply carry me along.
Everything seems so meaningless
and nothing appeals to my better instincts.
Help me to remember that Jesus gave
meaning
to everything in the world.

Let me bank on that fact
and get over this time of despair,
to really believe in the depths of my being
that there is a reason for living.
Show me the reason for my life
and tell me what I must do.
Bring home to me that I am never alone,
but that You are with me even in the
depths of despair.
Remind me that no matter what I may endure now

an unending joy awaits me in the future
if I but cling tightly to You
and Your Son Jesus in the unity of the
   Spirit.

Prayer in Time of Doubt

Lord Jesus,
I believe that You are the Son of God
and the Savior of the world.
Sometimes doubts assail me,
making me confused and frightened.
I know that this is because we still walk
in the shadows of faith while on earth,
relying on the testimony of those who have
   seen and believed.
But I am still affected to some extent
and somewhat shaken by such doubts.

Make me realize that our doubts are the
   price that we have to pay
for the fulfillment of the universe in Christ
and the very condition of that fulfillment.
We must be prepared to press on to the end
along a road on which each step makes us
   more certain,
toward horizons that are ever more
   shrouded in mists.
All the while we bring forth fruits worthy
   of our new life
such as charity, joy, and service of others.

In so doing we ourselves become for others
living signs of the power of Christ's resur-
    rection
which the Holy Spirit sets in motion in the
    Church.

Prayer before Driving

Dear Lord,
I am about to enter once again
into one of the amazing inventions of the
    human mind,
which You endowed with so much intelli-
    gence.
Yet like all human inventions and ad-
    vancement
it carries with it a negative side—
the risk of injury and even death
if it is misused whether deliberately or acci-
    dentally.

Help me to realize the responsibility that is
    mine
when I climb behind the wheel.
Let me drive defensively,
obeying the rules with care and alacrity
and avoiding the slightest act of mindless-
    ness.
Curb my anger when I am put in danger
by the carelessness of other drivers
and help me to maintain my balance.

Make my reflexes quick and my sight keen
so that I may react to any situation that
    may arise
and bring me safely (with my passengers)
    to my destination.

Prayer in Time of Dryness

Dear Lord,
I am enmeshed in a time of spiritual dry-
    ness.
You seem so far removed from me
and I cannot even pray.
I am deprived of all sensible consolations
which facilitate prayer and the practice of
    the virtues.
Yet I want to pray
and I want to remain close to You.

Let me realize the truth of the well-known
    axiom:
when we think God is furthest away from
    us
that is when He is closest to us.
Make me increase my efforts at prayer
even if I feel they are useless.
Keep me from being discouraged
and help me remain united with You.
Grant that I may regain my love for prayer
and grow in my relationship with You,

Your Son Jesus,
and the Holy Spirit.

Prayer in Time of Economic Hardship

Lord God,
it is symptomatic of our life today
that economics plays a large part in it.
People labor zealously for a wage
so that they can acquire the needs of life
for themselves and their families.
They also work for the so-called luxuries of
    life,
for the opportunity to have more leisure
to develop themselves in more ways,
and to keep up with their particular state
    of life.

Right now I find myself in a bad economic
    condition.
I just cannot seem to make enough money
to take care of myself and my family.
Please help me in this dangerous situation.
Teach me to live within my means
while at the same time striving to increase
    those means.
Let me never lose heart but continue to
    work on.
Most of all, inspire me to seek first Your
    Kingdom

in the knowledge that everything else will
   be given me
together with it.

Prayer in Time of Failure

Lord Jesus Christ,
I have just experienced the misfortune
of failing in some enterprise,
and I am overwhelmed by it.
Please grant me Your grace in this difficult
   time.
Let me realize that those who use all their
   talents
never fail in Your eyes.

In addition, assist me to see that You utilize our failures
to make us grow into better persons
and more devoted followers of You.
Make me recall that everything good comes
   from You,
indicating that I must work
as if everything depended on me
but pray as if it all depended on You.
Then if failure comes, there is a reason for
   it.
Help me to seek and find that reason
and live in accord with it.

Prayer of a Grateful Heart

Almighty God,
I thank You from the bottom of my heart
for this wonderful thing that has happened
   to me.
I know it is the result of Your goodness toward me
and I pray that I may accept it as I should.
In a world filled with many sufferings and
   sad occasions
I am fortunate to be blessed in this way.
I offer You my sincere gratitude
and promise to remain united with You
in good times and in bad.

Prayer in Time of Homesickness

Lord Jesus Christ,
I am far from home and family today
and afflicted with a bad case of homesick-
   ness.
Even though it is important and right for
   me to be away,
I miss my loved ones and my familiar surroundings.
Help me to realize that true Christians are
   never alone—
their spiritual family is ever with them:
You, the Father, and the Holy Spirit.

Let me dedicate myself anew to You today
thus overcoming this very human feeling
   within me.
Then help me to return home
with greater appreciation for my family
and for the things that I have from You.

Prayer in Time of Irritation

Lord God,
I am filled with irritation
over some occurrences that have taken
   place,
and it has led to a general impatience with
   things.
I get very unhappy with my lot
and with those closest to me.
Help me to overcome this feeling
and to cultivate a sense of patience.

Restore to me a sense of prayer
and of total confidence in You,
and enable me to accept whatever comes
with true Christian equanimity.
For after this life
You have reserved for Your children
a joy of unimaginable proportions.

Prayer in Time of Jealousy

Lord Jesus Christ,
I am caught in a web of jealousy

that stays with me night and day.
Help me to put away from me this evil
which Your Word tells us rots bones (Prov
14:30)
and even shortens lives (Sir 30:24).
Bring home to me the further evils
to which it leads if left unchecked:
slander, calumny, hatred,
damaged relations, persecutions, and
worse things.

Let me dwell constantly on the motives for
loving others
rather than being jealous of them.
Remind me of the fleeting character
of all life's attachments and successes
and of the fact that our true happiness
lies in being united closely with You
and with all others in You.

Prayer in Time of Joy

Lord of all goodness,
I am overcome with joy at this moment
because of the happy events that have oc-
curred
or simply because of the way You have
made us.
The world seems such a glorious place to
me
and all the cares of life seem far away.

Thank You for allowing such moments in
    our lives
and so giving us a glimpse of eternity.
I know that such a grand feeling is sure to
    pass
and that I will be once again confronted
with the problems and worries of daily life.
Let me realize that all true joy never fades,
for it is the gift of Your Spirit
made possible by the saving action of Your
    Son Jesus.
Keep me in Your grace
so that I may never lose that inner virtue of
    joy
even when the outward experience of joy
    has passed away.

Prayer in Time of Loneliness

Lord Jesus Christ,
I am assailed by a spell of loneliness.
All of a sudden it is as if I am totally alone,
without anyone in the world.
It is a terrifying feeling, Lord;
help me to overcome it.
Let me realize that I am never really alone
if I am united with You—
for You are always with me.

At the same time, remind me that I also
    have need of others,

for I am a social being.
And there are many people whom You
    have brought into my life
to help me on my way to eternity.
Teach me to see that we need one another
if we are to make a go of our lives
and complete the tasks You have given us.

Prayer for a Loving Attitude

Lord Jesus Christ,
You gave Your life out of love for all people
and You encouraged Your followers to do
    good to others.
Over the years many Christians have found
    this difficult
and I am no exception.
I try, but it is so hard
to have a loving attitude toward all—
and then I feel hypocritical in claiming to
    follow You.

Help me, dear Lord, to really believe
that Christian love is the greatest energy in
    the world.
Let me see that this is not an emotion
but a central attitude of one's being—
an attitude of service for others in Your
    Name.
It is the result of Your grace,
and prompts us to will only good things for
    others

as images of God.
Grant that I may always strive to attain
    this attitude
and so live up to the noble vocation to
    which I am called.

Prayer in Time of Mystical Insight

Lord Jesus Christ,
every once in a while You grant me the
    great gift
of an inspiring mystical insight
into some aspect of the Christian Faith.
It may happen in church or riding a bus,
walking down the street or sitting at home.
Invariably, it fills me with joy
at the thought of Your infinite love for me.

Thank You, dear Lord, for creating me,
redeeming me, and making me a Chris-
    tian.

Prayer in Time of Natural Disaster

Lord God,
a catastrophe happened today
and it has saddened me greatly.
Such evil presents a problem for all people
and I beg You to help me accept it
in the best way that I can.

I know that growth takes place only
    through risk
and it necessarily entails evils.

Let me dwell on the good You reserve for
us,
which will more than make up for the evil
we suffer here.
Help me to place myself in Your hands
and to accept whatever evils may come
in the firm knowledge
that they will lead me
more surely to You.

Prayer for a Sense of Humor

Lord Jesus Christ,
for some reason many Christians seem to
lack
a sense of humor.
They become so bogged down in the grav-
ity of things
that they are perpetually tense and serious-
minded.
Aid me to cultivate a sense of humor
and use it to help others as well as myself.
Let me realize that humor is also a creation
of Yours
and that a smile is one of the greatest blessings of life.
Teach me to stress the positive side of life
and develop a fine sense of humor.

Prayer in Time of Serenity

Eternal Lord,
it isn't often but once in a while
I experience a highly refined sense of serenity.
At such times I feel very close to You,
happy with my life
and ready to do anything asked of me.
I realize that these are moments of sensible consolation
and such consolation is never permanent—
still it is very nice to experience.

Grant me the grace to remain just as attached to You
when I am deprived of consolation.
Let me learn to concentrate on what is important.
in my relationship with You,
so that I may bear witness to You
in every circumstance of my life.

Prayer in Time of Sleeplessness

Lord Jesus Christ,
during Your earthly sojourn
You went sleepless at times
and spent whole nights in prayer.
But many other times You slept.
I cannot seem to get to sleep these nights
and I cannot even pray.

Please help me cure this sickness, Lord,
for I desperately need sleep to do my work
and to behave as a pleasant human being
as well as to act in a Christian manner.
Enable me to get a good night's sleep,
or at least to spend my time in prayer.

Prayer in Time of Success

Dear Lord,
You have been gracious enough
to allow me to score a great success.
I humbly thank You for Your help
and I hope that I will continue to receive it.
Let me never forget that without You
I would never have achieved anything.
True, I made use of my talents
but they were given to me by You,
and so was the drive to use them.

May I always strive to utilize all my talents
to the very best of my ability—
whether I achieve success or not.
For I will in this way be achieving the goal
that You have set out for me
and become the person You want me to be.

Prayer for the Virtue of Temperance

Lord Jesus Christ,
I tend to overdo almost anything.

When I am involved in something I plunge
into it
so that I am oblivious of everything else.
Give me a spirit of temperance
to maintain my balance in all things—
whether it be sleeping, thinking, or working,
playing, visiting, or partying.
Let me realize that whatever I do
I should do for You—and I should do it in
moderation!

Prayer in Time of Weariness

Lord God,
I am overcome with weariness and fatigue
both of body and of spirit.
I have been working doubly hard for a long
time
and I am beginning to feel the effects.
Let me take this as a sign from myself
that I must slow down,
cut down on pet projects,
and eliminate superfluous details.

Help me not to wait till it is too late.
Teach me how to continue to serve You
with a less hectic schedule
and a more sheltered life.

RECOURSE TO PRAYER IN SICKNESS AND SUF-FERING—When all else fails us, we can always count on prayer. For we know that God wants to help us and will always alleviate spiritual evil while sometimes also eliminating material evils. All we need do is ask with faith.

PRAYERS IN TIME OF SICKNESS AND SUFFERING

Christians have always regarded sickness and suffering as one of the ways in which we can best imitate our Lord Jesus Christ. When sickness strikes, it uproots us from our everyday life and our customary work schedule and makes us experience solitude and dependence on others as well as the fragile character of life. We are called to live this event too in faith.

While we struggle against the evil to conquer it, our Lord calls us to join our sufferings with His own in order to collaborate with Him on our salvation. Many times He does not free us from the sickness but He does something greater. He gives meaning to suffering and He opens our hearts to hope.

In order to unite themselves with Christ the sick have recourse to reception of the Sacraments (Anointing of the Sick, Penance, and the Eucharist) as well as private prayer. At such times it is difficult to pray, however. That is the reason why this section has been included herein. It provides prayers and ideas for prayers that can be said by the sick persons themselves.

The prayers are intended to inspire the sick to make good use of their temporary withdrawal from ordinary life, after the manner of Ignatius Loyola who made use of sickness to change his life and get closer to God, and Margaret of Cortona who made use of suffering to do the same.

Prayer of Resignation in Suffering

Merciful Lord of life,
I lift up my heart to You in my suffering
and ask for Your comforting help.
I know that You would withhold the thorns
    of this life
if I could attain eternal life without them.
So I throw myself on Your mercy,
resigning myself to this suffering.
Grant me the grace to bear it
and to offer it in union with Your sufferings.
No matter what suffering may come my
    way,
let me always trust in You.

Prayer To Accept Suffering

O my Lord Jesus Christ,
I believe . . . that nothing great is done
without suffering, without humiliation,
and that all things are possible by means of
  it.
I believe, O my God,
that poverty is better than riches,
pain better than pleasure,
obscurity and contempt than name,
and ignominy and reproach than
  honor. . . .
O my dear Lord,
though I am so very weak
that I am not fit to ask for suffering as a
  gift,
and have not strength to do so,
at least I would beg of Your grace
to meet suffering well,
when You in Your wisdom lay it upon me.

Cardinal Newman

Prayer of Offering of Suffering

Lord of all,
You created me
and most lovingly care for me.
I accept all my sufferings most willingly,

and as a truly obedient child I resign myself
to Your holy will.
Grant me the strength to accept generously
Your loving visitation,
and never let me grieve Your faithful heart
by giving in to impatience and discourage-
ment.

I offer You all my pains;
and in order that they may be acceptable to
You
and fruitful for my salvation
I unite them with the most bitter pains
of Your beloved Son Jesus.

Another Prayer of Offering
of Suffering

My Divine Savior, Jesus,
You loved me to such a degree
as to suffer and die for my salvation.
Through the love I have for You,
I most willingly offer to Your honor
all that I have ever suffered in the past,
am now suffering,
or will suffer in the future.
This is the basis and motive
of the love that animates me.
Your love enables me to suffer with joy.
I will to suffer because You suffered

and because You want me to suffer,
for I love you more than myself.

St. Gertrude

Prayer to Suffer in Union with Jesus

Dear Jesus,
for love of You
I desire to suffer all things,
because for love of me
You endured such cruel torments.
O my Jesus,
I unite my pains with the ones which You
    suffered
and I make an offering of them
to Your eternal Father.
O my Jesus,
out of the abundance of Your Divine goodness
give me the virtues of meekness and patience,
so that I may willingly carry my cross after
    You.

Prayer To Suffer in Silence

Lord Jesus Christ,
grant me the grace to be kind and gentle
in all the events of my life.
Let me put self aside
and think of the happiness of others.

Teach me to hide my little pains and disappointments
so that I may be the only one who suffers
for them.

Let me learn from the suffering that I must
endure.
May I so use it as to become
mellow rather than embittered,
patient rather than irritable,
and forgiving rather than overbearing.

Prayer of Acceptance of Sickness

Dear Lord,
I desire to accept this sickness from Your
hands
and to resign myself to Your will,
whether it be for life or for death.
Help me to be faithful to my desire
and give me the courage to carry it out.

Prayer for Help in Time of Sickness

Lord Jesus Christ,
Incarnate Son of God,
for our salvation
You willed to be born in a stable,
to endure poverty, suffering, and sorrow

throughout Your life,
and finally to experience the bitter death of
the Cross.

I beg you to say to Your Father on my be-
half:
"Father, forgive him/her."
At my death, say to me:
"This day you shall be with Me in
paradise."
And let me throw myself on Your mercy:
"Into Your hands I commend my spirit."

Prayer for the Restoration of Health

O Sacred Heart of Jesus
I come to ask You for the gift of restored
health
that I may serve You more faithfully
and love You more sincerely than in the
past.
I want to be well and strong
if it is Your will
and redounds to Your glory.

If on the other hand it is Your will
that my sickness continue,
I want to bear it with patience.

If in Your divine wisdom
I am to be restored to health and strength,
I will strive to show my gratitude
by a constant and faithful service rendered
  to You.

Prayer To Love God More Than Health

Almighty God,
You gave me health and I forgot You.
You take it away and I return to You.
How gracious You are to take away the
  gifts
that I allowed to come between You and
  me.
Take away everything that hinders my
  union with You.
Everything is Yours—
dispense comforts, success, and health
in accord with my real good.
Take away all the things
that displace my possession of You
so that I may be wholly Yours for time and
  eternity.

Prayer When Death Approaches

Most blessed and glorious Creator,
You have nourished me all my life
and redeemed me from all evil.
It is Your gracious will
to take me out of this fragile life
and to wipe away all tears from my eyes
and all sorrows from my heart.

I humbly consent to Your Divine plan
and I cast myself into Your sacred arms.
I am ready, dear Lord,
and earnestly expect and long for Your
good pleasure.
Come quickly and receive Your servant
who trusts completely in You.

Prayer of Consolation
with God's Word

Do not fear nor be dismayed,
for the Lord, your God, is with you
wherever you go. (Jos 1:9)
—The Lord is my shepherd; I shall want
for nothing . . .
I fear no evil; for You are at my side. (Ps
23)
—The Lord is my light and my salvation;
whom should I fear?

The Lord is my life's refuge;
of whom should I be afraid? (Ps 27)
—God is our refuge and our strength,
an ever-present help in distress. . . .
The Lord of hosts is with us;
our stronghold is the God of Jacob. (Ps 46)
—Bless the Lord, O my soul;
and forget not all His benefits;
He pardons all your iniquities,
He heals all your ills. (Ps 103)
—They carried to Jesus
all those afflicted and wracked with pain:
the possessed, the lunatics, the paralyzed.
He cured them all. (Mt. 4:24)
—Come to Me, all you who are weary
and find life burdensome,
and I will refresh you. (Mt 11:28)
—I am with you always,
until the end of the world. (Mt 28:20)
—I Myself am the living bread come down
  from heaven.
If anyone eats this bread he shall live forever;
the bread I will give is My flesh,
for the life of the world. (Jn 6:51)
—I came that they might have life
and have it to the full. (Jn 10:10)

—I am the resurrection and the life:
whoever believes in Me,
even though he should die, will come to
   life;
and whoever is alive and believes in Me
will never die. (Jn 11:25f)
—Do not let your hearts be troubled.
Have faith in God and faith in Me. (Jn
   14:1)

PRAYER DURING HOLIDAYS AND VACA-TIONS—A dedicated effort to maintain an active prayer life during holidays and vacations will return huge dividends. Our prayers will make our vacations more beneficial and our holidays more meaningful.

PRAYERS FOR HOLIDAYS
AND VACATIONS

No matter how it may appear at times, the life of every human being is not one long period of unremitting toil and struggle. It is interspersed by our compassionate Creator with periods of rest and recuperation. The rhythm of work-rest-sleep found in our daily experience is also found on a broader scale annually. The longer periods of rest are known as holidays and vacations.

During such times Christians usually have a golden opportunity to become refreshed for the ongoing struggle of life. They are times of new awakening, learning, travel, and leisure that restore our energies and our will to live. It is very important, therefore, that during such times we do not lose our spiritual momentum and neglect our devotional practices.

On holidays and during vacations, we should make a dedicated effort to maintain our prayer life so that we may be spiritually renewed also. Since our schedules at these times will be out of the usual and we may even be in different surroundings, we will find our prayer life difficult to maintain. However, if we set aside a few moments for reflection, we will be greatly blessed and spiritually renewed on our return to ordinary life.

The purpose of this section is to provide themes and ideas for prayers that will accord with holidays and vacations. The underlying point is that our union with the Father and Jesus in the Holy Spirit never takes a vacation. It may change direction and even experience adaptation, but it should remain ever solid and fruitful. Once again, the prayers found herein are only indicative and can easily give rise to others that will be more in conformity with one's individual circumstances.

Prayer on New Year's Day

Jesus, You are the Lord of history,
and Your wonderful redemption comes to
    us
in a cycle of time—year after year.
Now another year has passed
and a new one is ready to begin.
A backward glance tells us that last year
had its good points as well as its bad.

May the new year hold many more good
  things
in store for me
and make me a better person:
kinder and more willing to help,
more thoughtful and more loving.
May I fulfill my allotted task in life
and come closer to You
while looking forward to an eternity with
  You.
Thank You, Lord, for this extended time
that You so graciously allow me
on my journey toward Your heavenly
  Kingdom.

Prayer on Lincoln's Birthday

Almighty God,
today is the birthday of President Lincoln,
a man who was your chosen instrument
in the liberation of the black people.
Like Cyrus of old, Lincoln did not know
that Your Spirit was working through him,
yet he cooperated with Your grace
and achieved the task You set for him.

Teach me to see that same Spirit's hand
  working
in any human person, instrument or experience,
and to be able to use any event to work
  with You.

Let me strive to eliminate prejudice in myself
and in my circle of friends and acquaintances.
But let me insure that this will be done—
in Lincoln's beautiful phrase—
with malice toward none
and with charity for all.

Prayer on St. Valentine's Day

Lord of heaven,
You are known as the God of Love,
and today we are celebrating St. Valen-
tine—
one of the human patrons of love.
Teach me how to make use of the gift of
love
that You have given us,
and how to combine it with the supernatural virtue
that You infuse into us.
Let me love You above all
and others in and for You.

Make me faithful to my loved ones,
loyal, dedicated, compassionate, and concerned.
Let me overlook their human failings
and dwell on their good points.
Enable me to love them

not so much for what they can do for me
but for what I can do for them.

Prayer on Washington's Birthday

Dear Jesus,
today we celebrate the birthday
of the "Father of our country."
Amid many dangers and with much help,
this man forged a motley group into a free
   people
and left us a legacy of truthfulness.
Help me to realize that I am part of another people,
which You purchased by Your blood:
a chosen race, a royal priesthood, a holy
   nation,
a people of God.
Keep me faithful to this image
and make me relish the truth
after the example of Washington
and even more after Your own example,
for You said that "the truth will make you
   free."

Prayer on Martin Luther King Day

Lord of all,
today we honor the memory of a Christian
   minister
who put his Faith into practice
for the good of an oppressed people.

He followed Your evangelical counsel of non-violence
to overturn the discriminatory practices
of the ignorant and the misguided.

Teach me to put my Christianity into practice
in the cause of right wherever it may be
and for the freedom of blacks and other minorities.
Let me do what I can to insure that this country,
based on Christian principles,
will remain true to these principles and really be
"the land of the free and the home of the brave."

Prayer on Mother's Day

Almighty God,
You have been pleased to give all human beings
the joy of having a mother,
one who works with You to give them life
and bring them to human adulthood.
You have given followers of Your Son
the added joy of a Christian mother,
who works with You to give supernatural life to a a child

and bring up that child to Christian adulthood.

Over the centuries there have been countless such mothers—

heroic, courageous, loving, dedicated, and
unconquerable.

They have given us the Christian Ages and
Christian Saints

and in the final analysis the Christian
Faith.

Without them, there would be no Church,

no religious vocation, and no Christian influence in the world.

Most of these mothers are unsung in the
eyes of the world;

they must be content with little things:

a smile, a thank you, and a token remem-
brance.

In Your eyes, however, they are of inesti-
mable worth.

Your Word in the Bible uses a mother's
love

to describe Your overwhelming love for
Your people,

and Jesus uses the image of a mother bird

to indicate His love for His people.

Most of all, when He wants to convey an
idea

of the joy of those in heaven

He does so by using the image of a mother's
   pure joy
in bringing a child into the world.

Dear Lord,
let me honor my mother if she is living
and remember her in prayer if she is dead.
Pour down Your grace on her and all
   mothers
on this day dedicated to them.

Prayer on Memorial Day

Lord Jesus Christ,
today we honor the memory of those men
   and women
who have given their lives for their compa-
   triots
in the cause of freedom.
They have worked, fought, and died
for the heritage of freedom, brotherhood,
   and honor
that they have passed on to us.

Help us to recall that You Yourself
gave up Your life for all human beings
in the cause of true freedom—
to save us from self-love and sin.
Teach us the true meaning of peace and
   freedom,
that the real battle must always take place
   in ourselves

before it will be won in families and nations.

Make us keep Your memory in our
Eucharistic celebrations

and pray for the peace and freedom of the
whole world.

Prayer on Father's Day

Almighty God,

You have given us the wonderful gift of a
father after Your example.

Down through the ages fathers have cared
for their children

and most of them have given themselves
unstintingly for their families.

I thank You for my father:

even though he may not agree completely

with my outlook and way of life,

I know that he is genuinely concerned
about me.

Keep him well in body and soul

and if he has already come to You

grant him eternal happiness.

Dear Lord,

inspire all fathers to some of the virtues

toward their children

that You have toward us.

May all fathers watch over their children,

show kindness in their failings,

illumine their ignorance,
and encourage them in their just concerns,
thus leading them to a true Christian
  adulthood.

Prayer on a National Holiday

Lord of heaven,
You created me and made me
a citizen of this country
by birth (or by naturalization).
Let me take part in this holiday
with joy and gratitude.
As I am renewed in mind and body,
may I also be refreshed in spirit.

Make me take this occasion
to rededicate myself to my country
to lovingly uphold its legitimate traditions,
readily obey its decent laws,
and show genuine concern for its people.
At the same time, may I bear uncom-
  promising witness
of my Christian Faith to my fellow citizens
and to those who may not be followers of
  Jesus.

Prayer on Independence Day

Lord God,
like the Israelites of old, our ancestors in
  the faith,

our country has struggled long and hard to
  be free
and to keep its freedom as a nation.
It too has met with success and failure
in trying to achieve its goals.
Let me take this holiday celebration
to ponder the strengths and weaknesses of
  my country.
Make me resolve always to do my part to
  keep it strong
and strive constantly to eliminate its weaknesses:
in the social, political, economic, and religious field.

Teach me to meditate on the teachings of
  Your Son
Who brought us a message of peace and
  freedom
and instructed us to live as brothers and
  sisters.
His message took form in the vision of our
  founders
as they fashioned a nation
where people might live as one.
May this message live on in our midst
as a task for people today
and a promise for tomorrow.
Thank You for your past blessings
and for all that, with Your help, we will
  achieve in the future.

Prayer during Vacation Time

Dear Lord,
you have mercifully allowed human beings
  to have
periods of rest and recuperation
on our long journey through life.
This is my extended period of rest this
  year—
my vacation from the usual cares of everyday life
and my time to be renewed—
physically, mentally, and spiritually.

Grant that this vacation will bring me
a new awareness of the good things in life,
increased knowledge of Your wondrously
  versatile creativity,
delightful   travel   through   fascinating
  places,
and genuine leisure facilitating revitaliza-
  tion.
Let me be ever mindful of You
and my true goals in life.
And bring me back to carry out my daily
  tasks
with cheerfulness and goodwill,
and to the best of my strength and ability.

Prayer on Labor Day

Lord Jesus Christ,
it is the Christian religion based on Your
    teachings
that freed work from its degrading charac-
    ter
and made it into something noble—
so much so that is has become associated
with the so-called work-ethic,
symbolized by St. Paul's practical princi-
    ple:
"If anyone will not work, let him not eat!"
Let me realize that Christians work
in imitation of You and the Father
in accord with Your words:
"My Father has been working till now
and I work."

By work we build up the world,
as mentioned by the lines of a classic poem:
"God bless the noble working men
who rear the cities of the plain,
who dig the mines and build the ships,
and drive the commerce of the main.
God bless them! for their swarthy hands
have wrought the glory of our lands."

Let me also understand that work is good
because it builds up Your Body in the
    world
until Your second coming in glory.

Thus all human beings are called to work
no matter what type it may be—
from the homemaker to the secretary,
the teacher to the ditch-digger.
And, in reality, there is no difference to the
  worker—
all work is hard and yet fulfilling,
a burden but at the same time a psycho-
  logical necessity.
Most of all let me realize that no matter
  what work I do,
if I fail to do it,
no one else will—
and there will be a setback in building up
  Your Body.

Prayer on Columbus Day

God of love and majesty,
today we honor a brave explorer
who followed Your inspirations
and opened up a whole new world for all
  people.
He combined human vision with Divine
  faith,
human daring with Christian hope.

Grant me the grace to share in the virtues
  of Columbus
just as I share in the benefits of his journey
by living in the land he discovered.

In my own small way let me also conquer
    new worlds
by leading others to the knowledge of You
through a genuine Christian witness,
just as I share in the benefits of his journey.

Prayer on Election Day

Lord God,
in Your infinite wisdom
You gave human beings the power
to govern themselves in this world.
Those living in a democracy are fortunate
to have the privilege of self-determination
through regular election of leaders.
Help me to take full advantage of this priv-
    ilege
and never fail to cast my vote
for the best qualified person,
remembering that every vote counts.

Let me diligently analyze the issues and
    candidates
and then give my vote to the one
who is most in accord with Christian prin-
    ciples,
judging not so much by public utterances
    of candidates
as by their professional performances in
    office.

Help me to make the right choices
as I go to the polls today,
and send forth Your Spirit
to enlighten and guide those who are
   elected.

Prayer on Veterans Day

Dear Lord Jesus Christ,
those whom we honor today
are examples of your words:
"Greater love than this no one has:
that he lay down his life for his friends."
They gave up their lives in the defense of
   freedom
for their loved ones and their country.

Teach me to appreciate the virtue of
   patriotism—
a true and Christian love of country.
Let me love my country not to follow it
   blindly
but to make it the land of goodness
that it should be.
Let my patriotism be such
that it will not exclude the other nations of
   the world
but include them in a powerful love of
   country
that has room for all others too.

Prayer on Thanksgiving Day

Heavenly Father,
this is the day set aside to give You thanks
for Your surpassing goodness to human be-
    ings.
You have created us in Your own image
and set us over Your wonderful creation.
You chose a people to be Your own
and to carry Your message of salvation to
    all people.
You carried out Your redemption in Jesus
    Your Son,
and His saving fruits are passed on to every
    generation
to all who believe that by His Death and
    Resurrection
Jesus has given them a new freedom in His
    Spirit.

Let me give You proper thanks for Your
    blessings—
those I am aware of
as well as those that I habitually take for
    granted.
And let me learn to use them according to
    Your will.

CITIZENS OF WORLD AND COUNTRY

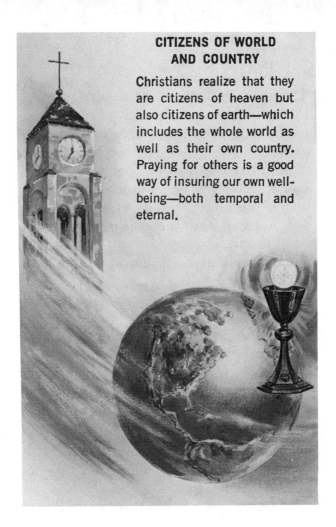

Christians realize that they are citizens of heaven but also citizens of earth—which includes the whole world as well as their own country. Praying for others is a good way of insuring our own well-being—both temporal and eternal.

PRAYERS FOR WORLD AND COUNTRY

We live in an age when the world has become a "global village." As soon as something happens anywhere in the world, it is made known to us through the magic of modern mass communications. Thus our awareness of others is heightened and all human beings are brought closer together.

It is only natural, then, for contemporary Christians to have a genuine interest in all that goes on daily throughout the world. This gives them a better opportunity than their ancestors for putting Christ's command of love into practice—for they have not a few but vast numbers of people to whom they can show love. They possess a golden opportunity to "do good to all men" (Gal 6:10) through their concern and their prayers, for in a certain sense each of us is a citizen of the world

However, this in no way lessens the attachment of Christians to their country of origin or citizenship. If anything, it solidifies and enlarges that attachment. They have a greater sense of being part of the whole human race—

but a very particular part, living in a specific land with its own traditions, laws, customs, and idiosyncrasies that can also be of help to others living in other lands.

Hence, Christians can legitimately pray for their country's welfare even as they pray for the welfare of all countries in the world. They can beseech God to make them good citizens of their country as well as upstanding members of the human race. For in the final analysis these two things go hand in hand. That is the whole thrust of the prayers found in this section — to foster a love for the world and for one's country.

Prayer for International Agencies

Lord God,
You created this vast and wonderful universe,
redeemed it in the blood of Your Son,
and now guide it by Your Holy Spirit.
It is Your will that we live as brothers and sisters,
building up the world by the marvelous powers
that You have graciously given us.

Look graciously on the representatives of
the nations
who are gathered together today for the
good of all.
Enlighten them to put forth wise proposals
in accord with Your will.
Teach them to deliberate with honesty
and with genuine respect for one another.
Help them to make just decisions
that will redound to the peace and welfare
of all nations.

Prayer for Good International Relations

Lord God,
enlighten the minds and open the hearts
of the statesmen of this world,
that they may make good relations flourish
between nations.

Keep them ever mindful of Your guiding
principles
to bring about true justice and peace
among peoples.

Let Your Spirit inspire them in their delib-
erations
and so lead to genuine harmony in the
world.

Prayer for the Full Development of All Peoples as Well as All Individuals

Almighty God,
in Your goodness
You have given human beings
the capacity to better their earthly lot
even as they make their way to You for
  eternity.
Grant that the true progress made till now
will not stop but be intensified
and eliminate the natural evils that still
  exist.
Fill the material needs of all who are deprived
even of the basic necessities of life
as well as the moral needs of those steeped
  in pride.
Let all people be freed from misery
and find subsistence and fulfilling work.
May every human being be able to do,
  know, and have more
in order to attain the self-fulfillment you
  desire.

Inspire everyone to know higher values,
to be open to Your grace and the gift of
  faith,
and to live in communion with You and the
  neighbor.

Prompt all persons to make regular use
of the means required to reach their own
full development
as well as the development of others.

Prayer for the Hungry

Lord Jesus Christ,
You urged us to give You food in Your
hunger
which is visible to us in the starving faces
of other human beings.
Let me realize that there are millions of
persons—
children of the same God and our brothers
and sisters—
who are dying of hunger
although they do not deserve to do so.

Do not allow me to remain indifferent
to their crying need,
or to soothe my conscience with the
thought
that I cannot do anything about this evil.
Help me to do something—
no matter how small—
to alleviate their heart-rending want.
At the very least, let me pray regularly
that these poor starving people will be re-
warded

for this terrible suffering they are enduring,
and be relieved of it as soon as possible.

Prayer for Sufferers throughout
the World

Lord Jesus Christ,
during Your life You were surrounded by
  suffering
and You eliminated it whenever You
  could.
Look down on this suffering world
and alleviate all its suffering.
Help the sick in body, especially those ter-
  minally ill,
and the sick at heart who are weary of life.
Come to the aid of those victimized by war
or by their uncaring neighbors.
Encourage those who suffer discrimination
because of race, creed, or color,
because of their poverty, ignorance, or different life-style.
Free those who are oppressed
and feed those who are hungry.
Inspire in me a firm desire to cooperate
  with You
in this liberation of the downtrodden.
Let me be open to others,
to love them in You
and share with them what I am and have.

Prayer for Peoples at War

Lord God,
the peoples of two nations are suffering
the terrible ravages of war.
Their loved ones are imperiled by death,
their lives are in danger of being shattered,
their spirits are slowly becoming embittered,
and their souls are endangered by unrelenting hatred.

Pour forth Your grace on these peoples.
Keep their hearts centered on You
and lead their minds away from the evils of war.
Let all pray and work for peace,
so that their lives may return to normal
and they can worship You in faith, hope, and love.
Remove the horrors of war from their midst
and bring them the benefits of peace.

Prayer for Disarmament

Almighty God,
You want to save us from the age-old slavery of war.
Yet at the present time we are engaged in an arms race
that seems to be the only deterrent to war.

Inspire leaders of nations to find an alter-
    native method
for as the Second Vatican Council has said,
it is not a safe way to preserve peace.
Nor is the so-called balance that results
    from it
a sure and authentic peace.
Enable us to find new approaches
and to restore genuine peace based on Your
    law
thus emancipating the world from its
    crushing anxiety.

Prayer for Openness to the World

Lord Jesus Christ,
You came into this world as a man
and took part in the customs of Your day.
By so doing You showed us
that we can be fully and genuinely human
only by following You.
Help us to be open to the world
in a truly Christian manner.

Let the joys and hopes, sorrows and anx-
    ieties
of all who live in this age
be our joys and hopes, sorrows and an-
    xieties
as your disciples.

May nothing that is really human
fail to find an echo in our hearts.
Teach me to apply Your principles
to the world events that I encounter each
  day.
Let me never flee from this world
but bring You into it every day of my life.

Prayer for the Godless

O Almighty God,
You have given us faith in Christ
as a beacon to light our way
amid the darkness of the world.
Have mercy on all who have strayed
from the path of salvation
even though they may not know it.
Send Your message into their hearts
and grant them the grace to receive it
with sincerity and thankfulness.

Prayer for Our Country

Heavenly Father,
You are the real foundation of nations,
raising them up to serve and care
for the people dwelling in their boundaries.
I thank You for making me a citizen of this
  land
of freedom and unlimited opportunity—
which are the result of its Christian base.

Send forth Your Spirit to this country
and make it a source of wisdom and
   strength,
order and integrity throughout the world.

Prayer for Civil Authority

Lord Jesus Christ, King of the universe,
look with mercy on those who rule over us.
Grant to our President and his administra-
   tion
the grace to know and do Your will.
Let them serve all their subjects
in truth and righteousness.
Inspire our Congressmen with the courage
to make laws for the good of all
rather than the few.
Give our judges Your Spirit of wisdom and
   understanding
that they may discern the truth
and impartially administer the law.
And let all the people pitch in
to make our way of government continue
   to work.

Prayer for the Proper Use of Creation

Almighty God,
Creator of all things,
You made this earth

with its atmosphere and its myriad living
beings
in a marvelous and mind-boggling fashion
so that it could give birth and growth to humans.
You entrusted its environment and its resources to us
to be used in forging a life
that would bring us close to You
and eventually lead us to Your heavenly
Kingdom.

Help us to use these precious resources
with wisdom and restraint,
avoiding waste, pollution, and wanton de-
struction.
Make us act responsibly so that those who
follow us
will also be able to use the earth in Your
service.

Prayer for Social Justice

Lord God,
even in the Old Testament
as shown by those marvelous prophets
Amos and Hosea
Your message stressed the need for Your
servants
to effect social as well as individual justice
in the world.

Your Divine Son took the same message
even further,
calling for social charity as well.
And Your modern Popes have all stressed
social justice
if there is to be peace among people and
nations.
Grant me the grace to fight social evils and
oppression
even as I struggle against evil in myself.
Make me use my freedom according as
You will
in the pursuit of justice and peace
for Your honor and glory.

Prayer for Social Service

Lord Jesus Christ,
I know that Your call never comes to me in
a vacuum
but in the circumstances of my daily life.
Hence, my response cannot be given
only in the privacy of my own mind;
it must overflow into my daily life.
You call me through my family,
through my community or Church,
and through the world.

Teach me to serve others in the knowledge
that those actions of mine which advance
true progress

of the Church and the world
are my way of saying yes to Your call.
At the same time, let me take the opportunity
to make Your Gospel known through my actions
as I work with them to build the temporal order,
directing it to You Who are its final goal.

Prayer for the Advancement of Learning

Almighty God,
Your knowledge is infinite
and You have given human beings a wonderful capacity
to learn on every level:
practical, social, cultural, intellectual, and so on.
Bless all institutions of learning
and all teachers as well as all students.
Grant to them all as well as to me.
a dedication to true knowledge,
a true love of learning,
and a capacity to continue to learn throughout life,
until they arrive at the knowledge of You,
and Your Son, Jesus, in the unity of the Holy Spirit.

Prayer for the Proper Use
of the Means of Communication

Almighty God,
enable us to make proper use
of the marvelous means of communication
that are constantly being placed at our dis-
    posal
so that we will experience no harm,
and, like salt and light,
will give savor to the earth
and brighten the world.

May all men and women of good will
also strive to use them
solely for the good of society
whose fate depends more and more on
    their proper use.
Grant that, as was the case with ancient
    works of art,
these discoveries may serve to glorify
the Name of the Lord,
in accord with the words of the Apostle:
"Jesus Christ, yesterday and today,
and the same forever!"

Prayer for Industry

O God,
You have called us to cooperate by our
    daily work
in the immense plan of Your creation.

Give all of us a pride in what we do
and a just return for our labor.
Enable us to expand our activity with a
    Christian spirit,
in the awareness that every person is our
    brother or sister.
Grant that in the common effort
to build a more just and faithful world
all persons may find a place suited to their
    dignity
to fulfill their own vocation
and to contribute to the progress of all.

MEMBERS OF UNIVERSAL CHURCH THROUGH LOCAL CHURCH—Christians are members of the universal Church through membership in their local Church—parochial, diocesan, and national. As such, it is fitting that they pray for the whole Church as well as their own community.

108

PRAYERS FOR CHURCH AND PARISH

*A*s already mentioned, contemporary Christians have a greater awareness of their relationship to the world. They should also possess a corresponding awareness of their relationship to the universal Church and more specifically to the local Church (diocese) or parish (which is the smallest part of the diocesan and national Church). For in the wake of the Second Vatican Council, we are living in the age of the local Church.

In God's providence it is the Church which has the Holy Spirit in her that puts us in touch with Jesus and the salvation He has achieved. The Church is the sacrament of salvation for the entire world throughout the ages until Christ's final coming in glory.

In the case of individual Christians, it is ordinarily the Parish Church that puts them in touch with Jesus and His saving actions. It is the Parish Church where they can co-celebrate the Eucharistic celebration with their co-parishioners, where they receive the other sacraments, and where they carry out the religious tasks given them by God.

In the aftermath of Vatican II, the local Church has come into its own, bursting with committees and projects in which parishioners can take part and really pull their weight in the Church. The measure of their commitment to such tasks will determine the extent of the Church's influence in their lives.

Thus, Christians should make it a practice to pray for the needs of both the universal and the local Church. In doing so, they will call down God's grace on their Church and increase their own awareness of commitment to that Church.

Prayer for the Church

Come, Holy Spirit, blest Sanctifier,
mercifully assist Your Catholic Church.
By Your heavenly power
strengthen and establish her against the assaults
of her enemies.
By Your love and grace
renew the spirit of Your servants
whom You have anointed.

Grant that they may in You
glorify the Father and His only Son,
Jesus Christ our Lord.

Alternate Prayer for the Church

Heavenly Father,
grant that Your Church may always find
in the risen Jesus,
Who conquered death and sin,
the strength to overcome patiently and lov-
    ingly
all afflictions and hardships.
May she thus show forth in the world
the mystery of the Lord
in a faithful though shadowed way,
until at the last it will be revealed in total
    splendor.

Prayer for Deacons

Father of all,
You inspired the Twelve
to seek men of good repute,
filled with the Spirit and wisdom,
to be appointed to the task of service.
Pour out blessings in abundance on all
    Deacons,
their families, their ministry and service.
Grant that they may be filled with Grace
    and power
as they work among the people.

Prayer for the Local Church

God our Father,
Your Second Vatican Council has told us
that the Church of Christ is truly present
in all legitimate local congregations which,
united with their pastors,
are themselves called churches in the New
    Testament.
Let all such local churches
manifest Your universal Church—
One, Holy, Catholic, and Apostolic.
Grant that their members may grow
through the Gospel and the Eucharist
in the unity of the Holy Spirit.
Make them the genuine instrument of
    Christ's power in the world.

Another Prayer for the Local Church

Heavenly Father,
look graciously on the Church in our coun-
    try
and keep it faithful to Your Divine mes-
    sage.
Make it communicate that message in ways
that will be understood by our people
in terms of their culture and customs.
Inspire our religious leaders

with wisdom and courage in this important
   task.
At the same time enable all members of this
   Church
to answer Your call to spread their faith
among their fellow citizens.
Help us all to keep our Church ever full
of Your grace and Your teachings
and alive to the needs of all who are in
   need—
both materially and spiritually—
in imitation of Your Divine Son
and under the impulse of Your Holy Spirit.

Prayer for the Diocese

Heavenly Father,
in calling us to follow Christ Your Son
You have made us members of this diocese,
   which is a local Church.
Teach us to serve You faithfully in its
   boundaries
and to make it manifest the universal
   Church for us.
Help both religious and laity who form part
   of it
to work together in true Christian unity.

May Your Word be truly proclaimed and
   heard here

and may Your Sacraments, especially the
Eucharist,
be faithfully administered and devoutly received.
Grant that our diocese may provide a fer-
vent example
of the power of Your Word and the might
of Your salvation
for Your honor and glory and our salvation.

Prayer for the Parish

Heavenly Father,
You have chosen the parish as the vehicle
by which You encounter us in our daily
lives.
The parish is the assembly in which
Your Word is proclaimed,
Your Eucharist is celebrated,
Your people are united in a local community
and subdivided into smaller groups
so that they may become the agent of
change
for the betterment of the whole Church.
Make our parishioners aware
of the many opportunities and responsibilities

that are theirs as witnesses of You to our
   age.
Keep us open to our need of Your love and
   fellowship.
Let both religious and laity work together
to serve You in others.

Prayer for the Pope

Lord Jesus Christ,
You willed to build Your Church on Peter
   the Rock
and the Popes who have succeeded him
   through the ages.
Pour forth Your grace on our Holy Father
that he may be a living sign and an
   indefatigable promoter
of the unity of the Church.

Help him to proclaim Your message to all
   people
and to listen to the message that comes to
   him
from the consensus of all its members
and from the world that You made.
Make him serve others after Your example
and in accord with his traditional title:
"Servant of the servants of God."
Unite us closely to him
and make us docile to his teachings.

Prayer for the Bishop

Lord Jesus Christ,
You sent Your Apostles to proclaim the
  Good News
with Peter at their head
and You strengthened them with the Holy
  Spirit.
Remind us that our bishops are appointed
by that same Spirit
and are the successors of the Apostles
as pastors of souls.
Together with the Pope and under his authority
they have been sent throughout the world
to continue Your work.

Help our bishop to teach all members of his
  diocese,
to sanctify them in the truth,
and to give them Your nourishment.
Help us obey his teachings and love him
as the Church obeys and loves You.
May we remain united with him,
grow in faith and love,
and attain eternal life with You.

Prayer for All Church Leaders

Lord Jesus Christ,
watch over those who are leaders

in Your Church.
Keep them faithful to their vocation
and to the proclamation of Your message.
Teach them to recognize and interpret
the signs of the times.
Strengthen them with the gifts of the Spirit
and help them to serve their subjects,
especially the poor and lowly.
Give them a vivid sense of Your presence
in the world
and a knowledge of how to show it to
others.

Prayer for Priests

Heavenly Father,
pour out Your grace on the priests You
have made.
Let them remember that in performing
their tasks
they are never alone.
Relying on Your almighty power
and believing in Christ
Who called them to share in his priesthood,
may they devote themselves to their ministry
with complete trust,
knowing that You can intensify in them
the ability to love.

Let them also be mindful that they have as partners
their brothers in the priesthood
and indeed the faithful of the entire world.
For they cooperate in carrying out the saving plan of Christ,
which is brought to fulfillment only by degrees,
through the collaboration of many ministries
in the building up of Christ's Body
until the full measure of His manhood is achieved.

Prayer for a Parish Council

Lord Jesus Christ,
inspired by the words of Your Second Vatican Council,
we have elected some men and women of our parish
to the parish council.
These have the task to represent us
with the parish team
and to work for the good of the entire community.

Help them to carry out their role
with courage and wisdom,
with joy and dedication,

with patience and mutual respect,
and with the conviction that all they do
is done primarily for You
and the honor of the Blessed Trinity.

Prayer for a Spiritual
or Pastoral Meeting

Lord Jesus Christ,
we have come together in Your Name
to work for the good of this parish.
Stay with us with Your invisible presence
and pour out the gifts of Your Spirit on us.
Make us work in a spirit of trust and love,
as well as a spirit of prudence and under-
    standing,
so that we may experience an abundance
of light, compassion, and peace.
Let harmony reign ever among us
and let us keep our eyes ever fixed upon
    You.
Enable us to implement Your known will
    for us,
no matter what difficulty it may entail.

Prayer for a Study Group

Heavenly Father,
send forth Your Spirit
to enlighten our minds and dispose our
    hearts
to accept Your truth.

Help us to listen to one another
with openness and honesty,
eager to learn from the talents and intuitions
that You have given each of us.
Never let differences of opinion
diminish our mutual esteem and love.
May we leave this meeting
with more knowledge and love for You
and Your Son in the unity of the Holy
    Spirit.

Prayer for the Laity

Heavenly Father,
inspire all lay members of Your Church
to know their calling and carry it out.
Let them realize that they are to be witnesses
to Christ in all things
and in the midst of human society.

Help them to bear this witness
by their life and work in their home,
in their social group,
and in their professional circle.
Enable them to do so and thus radiate the
    new person
created according to God
in justice and true holiness (cf. Eph 4:24),

and so lay the groundwork for the growth
of Your Kingdom on earth.

Prayer for Priestly Vocations

O Jesus, Divine Pastor of souls,
You called the Apostles
to make them fishers of human beings,
Continue to draw to You
ardent and generous souls of Your people
to make them Your followers and minis-
    ters;
enable them to share Your thirst for uni-
    versal redemption
through which You daily renew Your sac-
    rifice.

O Lord,
always living to make intercession for us,
open the horizons of the whole world
where the mute supplication of so many
    hearts
begs for the light of truth and warmth of
    love.
Responding to Your call,
may they prolong Your mission here
    below,
build up Your mystical Body,
which is the Church,
and be the salt of the earth
and the light of the world.   *Pope Paul VI*

Prayer for Religious Vocations

O God,
You bestow gifts on human beings
for the upbuilding of Your Church
and the salvation of the whole world.
Pour out Your Spirit
to inspire young people
with the desire to follow You more closely
by embracing the Evangelical Counsels
of poverty, chastity, and obedience.

Grant Your powerful and continuing assistance
to all who respond to Your call
so that they may remain faithful to their vocation
throughout their lives.
May it lead them to greater fullness
and make them living signs of the new person in Christ,
freed from money, pleasure, and power,
and outstanding witnesses of Your Kingdom.

Prayer for Missionaries

Lord Jesus Christ,
watch over Your missionaries—
priests, religious, and lay people—
who leave everything

to give testimony
to Your Word
and Your love.
In difficult moments
sustain their energies,
comfort their hearts,
and crown their work
with spiritual achievements.
Let the adorable image
of You crucified on the Cross,
which accompanies them throughout life,
speak to them of heroism,
generosity,
love and peace.   *Pope John XXIII*

For Unity of Christians

Almighty and eternal God,
You keep together those You have united.
Look kindly on all who follow Jesus Your
    Son.
We are all consecrated to You by our com-
    mon Baptism;
make us one in the fullness of faith
and keep us one in the fellowship of love.

PRAYERS FOR FAMILY AND NEIGHBOR-HOOD—Prayer for one's family is so obvious that we tend to take it for granted most of the time and fail to use numerous opportunities for prayer that relate to the family. The same can be said for one's neighborhood. We should strive to remedy this lack.

PRAYERS FOR FAMILY AND NEIGHBORHOOD

In addition to their relationship to their country and their Church, all Christians have a close relationship to their families and to their local neighborhoods. In the normal course of things, these relationships also entail responsibilities and privileges as far as prayer is concerned.

The family has been termed a domestic Church, for it is called upon to form Christ in all its members. Indeed, for most Christians it is the place where they first encounter Christ through the prayers and example of their parents. Here too they gain their first experience of human Christian companionship and of the Church. It is only natural then that prayer should come to mind in relation to members of that family and the various occasions of their lives.

The family is also the springboard that gradually introduces human beings into civic partnership with their fellow humans. All Christians form part of a particular local neighborhood with customs and problems of its own.

"They must be acquainted with this culture, heal and preserve it. They must develop it in accordance with modern conditions, and finally perfect it in Christ" (Vatican II: Decree on the Missionary Activity of the Church, *no. 21). Under such circumstances, it is incumbent on Christians to pray for their immediate neighbors and their local surroundings when occasions arise that call for such prayer.*

The prayers found in this section cover only a few such occasions. Many others could be found but they would be too diversified because of the necessarily concrete circumstances that would have to be mentioned. Thus they will have to be left to the ingenuity of each person for composition. The prayers given offer a sufficient variety for such composition as the occasions arise.

Prayer for a Family

Jesus, our most loving Redeemer,
You came to enlighten the world
with Your teaching and example.
You willed to spend the greater part of
    Your life

in humble obedience to Mary and Joseph
in the poor home of Nazareth.
In this way You sanctified that family
which was to be an example for all Christian families.

Graciously accept our family
which we dedicate and consecrate to You
  this day.
Be pleased to protect, guard, and keep it
in holy fear, in peace,
and in the harmony of Christian charity.
By conforming ourselves to the Divine
  model
of Your family,
may we all attain to eternal happiness.

Another Prayer for a Family

God of goodness and mercy,
to Your fatherly protection we recommend
  our family,
our household, and all that belongs to us.
Fill our home with Your blessings
as You filled the holy house of Nazareth
with Your presence.
Keep us from sin.
Help each one of us to obey Your holy
  laws,
to love You sincerely, and to imitate Your
  example,

the example of Mary, Your mother and
ours,
and the example of Your holy guardian,
St. Joseph.

Lord, preserve us and our home
from all evils and misfortunes.
May we ever be resigned to Your Divine
will
even in the crosses and sorrows
which You allow to come to us.
Finally, give all of us the grace
to live in harmony and love toward our
neighbor.
Grant that each of us may deserve by a
holy life
the comfort of Your Sacraments at the
hour of death.

Bless this house,
God the Father, Who created us,
God the Son, Who suffered for us on the
Cross,
and God the Holy Spirit, Who sanctified us
at Baptism.
May the one God in three Divine Persons
preserve our bodies,
purify our minds,
direct our hearts,
and bring us all to everlasting life.

Litany for the Home

O Father in heaven,
we thank You for our home and our health;
—we thank You, Father.
For giving us to one another in this family,
for our happy family life together,
and comfort in our common sorrows,
—we thank You, Father.
We ask You to lead us
in the ways of love and service to one an-
    other;
—Lord, hear our prayer.
That with honesty and cheerfulness,
with bravery and truth,
we may be quick and ready to help each
    other
in each day's work and cares,
—Lord, hear our prayer.
That we may with respect and love
avoid quarrels in our home which would
    threaten unity,
and confine our differences in the home,
—Lord, hear our prayer.
For our life at home now,
and the memories to come,
for making us one and keeping us secure,
—we bless You, O God, our Father.

For the constant support of our holy
  Church worldwide,
for the assurance of graces given,
and for the promise of eternal peace,
—we thank You, O God, our Father.

Prayer of Parents for Their Children

Heavenly Creator of the universe,
we thank You for the children
that You have entrusted to us.
We want to cooperate with You fully
in helping them grow into free and respon-
  sible persons
and mature in the faith received at Baptism.
Grant us the grace to be able to guide them
in the practice of virtue
and the way of Your commandments—
by the good example of our lives,
and by the loving observance of Your law
and that of Your Church.
Most of all, however, guide them with
  Your Spirit
so that they may know the vocation You
  will for them
and be open to genuine self-giving and true
  Christian love.

Prayer of Children for Their Parents

Lord Jesus Christ,
You have given me my parents
to bring me into this world
and to help me on my journey to You in the
    next
by the consoling gift of Your holy and
    generous love.
Fill them with Your choicest blessings
and enrich their souls with Your grace.

Grant that they may faithfully and con-
    stantly imitate
Your mystical marriage to the Church
which You imprinted on them on their
    wedding day.
Inspire them with Your wisdom
and enable them to walk in the way of
    Your commandments.
And may I and their other children be ever
their joy in this life
and their crown of glory in the next.
Bring my parents to a ripe old age
in health of mind and body
and grant them a holy death in union with
    You.

Prayer of Spouses for One Another

Lord Jesus Christ,
help us to love each other

as You love Your Immaculate Bride, the
    Church.
Bestow on us Christian forbearance and
    patience
in bearing each other's shortcomings.
Let no misunderstanding disturb that har-
    mony
which is the foundation of mutual help
in the many and various hardships of life.

Inspire us to lead truly Christian lives
and cooperate with the sacramental grace
    given us
on our wedding day.
Give us the grace to live together in peace
    and happiness,
slow to speak harshly
and quick to forgive each other.
Enable us to rear our children in Your love,
assist our neighbor after Your example,
shoulder our rightful civic and religious
    burdens
in union with You,
and bear witness to You before our com-
    munity.

Prayer of Spouses on a
Wedding Anniversary

Almighty God,
we thank You from the bottom of our
    hearts

for Your continued blessings on our union
that have enabled us to reach another an-
    niversary.
We thank You for letting our love deepen
and for helping us in time of trial.
We know that without Your assistance
we would never have remained so close as
    we are.

We ask You to continue to watch over us,
over our homes and families.
Help us to renew our vows of love and loy-
    alty
and to strive to remain united with You,
steadfast in our Faith and in Your service.

Prayer at a Child's Baptism

Lord Jesus Christ,
You have given new birth to our child
by water and Your Holy Spirit.
You have made him/her a child of Your
    Father,
a member of Your Church,
and an heir of heaven.

We offer You sincere thanks
and promise with the help of Your grace
to teach him/her in accord with the baptis-
    mal promises

to believe unhesitatingly in Your message,
to obey faithfully Your commandments,
and to remain ever united with You
in life and in death.

Prayer for an Unwed Mother

Lord of life,
look graciously on this young woman
who has become a mother out of wedlock.
Grant her and her child Your strength
that they may grow in stature, age, and
    grace.
Inspire others to extend kindness and
    understanding
to them in their troubled lives,
so that they can live relatively peacefully.
Send them a good man who will be
a loving husband and father.
Teach me to put away all recrimination
    and condemnation
and be of help and encouragement to them.

Prayer at a Child's First Communion

Lord Jesus Christ,
in the Sacrament of the Eucharist
You left us the outstanding manifestation
of Your limitless love for us.
Thank You for giving our child

the opportunity to experience this love
in receiving the Sacrament for the first
time.
May Your Eucharistic presence keep him/
her
ever free from sin,
fortified in faith,
pervaded by love for God and neighbor,
and fruitful in virtue,
that he/she may continue to receive You
throughout life
and attain final union with You at death.

Prayer at the Confirmation of a Child

Almighty God,
You sent Your Spirit to transform the
Apostles
into heroes of evangelical strength
on the day of Pentecost.
Thank You for granting that same Spirit
to our child in the Sacrament of Confirma-
tion.
Pour down upon him/her
the sevenfold gifts of the Spirit
that he/she may more closely resemble
Jesus
and be an intrepid witness in the world
to You and to Your Divine Son.

Prayer at the Marriage of a Son or Daughter

Lord Jesus Christ,
You said that on their marriage
grown children should leave father and mother
and cling to their spouse.
Our child has taken this step today,
receiving the wonderful Sacrament of Marriage.

Watch over him/her in this new life.
May this couple find happiness in each other
and in You
as they raise a new family to Your honor and glory.
Help me to accept this marriage wholeheartedly
with the realization that I am not losing one child
but gaining another.

Prayer at a Child's Entrance into the Religious Life

Lord God,
You have called my son/daughter to be
a priest (or sister or brother),

and he/she has generously responded to
that call.
I pray that he/she will be ever faithful
in this new`state
and happy with the way of life lying ahead.

Help me to be ever ready to render my assistance
whenever and however it may be needed.
Let me always remember that it is an honor
to give one's child to You
Who gave it to us in the first place.

Prayer for a Child's Return
to the Faith

Dear Lord,
You became man, suffered, and died
to win salvation for all souls.
Look graciously on the soul of my child
who has drifted away from You and the
Faith.
Grant him/her Your grace
to see the error of his/her ways
and return to the fold in Your care.
Teach me to stay close to him/her
during this trying time
and strive to convert him/her by action and
prayers
more than by words that may antagonize.

Sacred Heart of Jesus, I trust You
to do everything to bring my child back to
    You.

Prayer for a Neighborhood
Civic Association

Lord Jesus Christ,
You praised those who serve the needs of
    others.
Look graciously on this neighborhood civic
    association
made up of people of various beliefs
who work for the good of our community.
Prompt them to show genuine respect for
    all
and to strive to eliminate all injustice
from our area.
Inspire its officers to perform their duties
    well
and the members to accept their leader-
    ship,
so that the people will be relieved of social
    concerns
and be better able to pursue their spiritual
    goal.

Prayer for a Neighborhood Problem

Heavenly Lord,
You know the problem that has arisen in
    our midst.

Please help those involved to resolve it
with all speed and according to Your will.
Watch over us with Your grace
so that this community will be a place
where Your presence is felt,
true human and Christian friendship
    reign,
and all work out their salvation in peace.

Prayer for a Declining Neighborhood

Lord Jesus Christ,
our neighborhood was once a thriving area
where people lived peaceful human lives
and fruitful spiritual lives.
Now it is in a state of continuous decline,
where peace and harmony have given way
to fear, suspicion, and chaos.
Inspire those who remain to refrain from
    fleeing
and to work together to build it up again.
Make us all respect one another
as we strive to restore our neighborhood
    into a place
where people can live in peace
and worship without fear.

Prayer for a Neighborhood School

Almighty God,
You have made human beings in such a
    way

that all education is most important for
their welfare.
Our neighborhood school is presently in a
sad state
and can barely teach our youngsters the es-
sentials
they need in order to live in union with
others
and with You, their Creator.
Help us to restore it to its former state
so that our children may receive a good
education
and be able to come to the knowledge of
You
and of Your Son—
which is eternal life.

Prayer for a Neighbor in Difficulty

Lord Jesus Christ,
You taught us to help those in need.
I pray for N. our neighbor who is in difficulty.
Watch over him/her during this time of
trial
and enable him/her to rebound from this
blow.
Most important of all, keep him/her close
to You
no matter what he/she may have to undergo.

Move me to do what I can to help
always respecting his/her privacy
and without in any way diminishing his/
    her own self-respect.

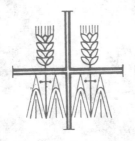

PRAYERS FOR SELF AND FRIENDS—There are countless occasions for prayer in our relationships with ourselves arnd with our friends. All that is needed is an awareness that whatever we may be doing Jesus is with us. We can tune Him in at any time and on any occasion.

PRAYERS FOR SELF AND FRIENDS

In addition to the relationships already mentioned, Christians also have a relationship to themselves as individuals. Jesus said: "Love your neighbor as yourself." Hence, Christians must do for themselves what they do for others. They must pray for themselves or see to it that their own prayer life does not suffer or become completely non-existent. They must afford spiritual help to themselves even as they do for others.

One of the ways to do this is to have a regular pattern of daily prayer—and that is the reason why we give set-time prayers in this section. Another way is to pray in any situation that may arise during the day. This leads to those prayers that we have already given in the section on states-of-mind prayers, but since there is a little different emphasis in this case we also give here a few such prayers.

Christians also have a relationship with friends and acquaintances. This naturally leads to prayer for such people. It is good for us to do this because

*it keeps before our eyes our depen-
dence on others and ultimately on our
Creator. At the same time it keeps us in
touch with Him.*

*By sanctifying our relationships we
become better able to cope with them
and to live a genuine Christian life.
Thus, nothing that we do becomes ordinary or secular. We live in tune with a
loving Father Who wants to help us at
every circumstance. By praying we
take advantage of that relationship
and we uncover the key to our universe.*

Morning Prayer

Most holy and adorable Trinity,
one God in three Persons,
I praise You and give You thanks
for all the favors You have bestowed on
    me.
Your goodness has preserved me until
    now.
I offer You my whole being
and in particular all my thoughts, words,
    and deeds,
together with all the trials I may undergo
    today.
Give them Your blessing.

May Your Divine Love animate them
and may they serve Your greater glory.

I make this morning offering
in union with the Divine intentions of Jesus
  Christ
Who offers Himself daily in the Sacrifice of
  the Mass
and in union with Mary, His Virgin Mother
  and our Mother,
who was always the faithful handmaid of
  the Lord.

Midafternoon Prayer

O Divine Savior,
I transport myself in spirit to Mount Cal-
  vary
to ask pardon for my sins,
for it was because of humankind's sins
that You chose to offer Yourself in sacrifice.
I thank You for Your extraordinary
  generosity
and I am also grateful to You
for making me a child of Mary, Your
  Mother.
Blessed Mother, take me under your protection.
St. John, you took Mary under your care.

Teach me true devotion to Mary, the
    Mother of God.
May the Father, the Son, and the Holy
    Spirit
be glorified in all places
through the Immaculate Virgin Mary.

Evening Prayer

I adore You, my God,
and thank You for having created me,
for having made me a Christian,
and for having preserved me this day.
I love You with all my heart
and I am sorry for having sinned against
    You,
because You are infinite Love and infinite
    Goodness.
Protect me during my rest
and may Your love be always with me.
Eternal Father,
I offer You the precious Blood of Jesus
    Christ
in atonement for my sins
and for all the intentions of our holy
    Church.
Holy Spirit, Love of the Father and the
    Son,
purify my heart and fill it with the fire of
    Your Love,

so that I may be a chaste Temple of the
   Holy Trinity
and be always pleasing to You in all things.

Prayer before Meals

Bless us, O Lord,
and these Your gifts
which we are about to receive
from Your bounty
through Christ our Lord.

Prayer after Meals

We give You thanks, Almighty God,
for all Your blessings:
Who live and reign for ever and ever.
   Amen.

Prayer for Jesus' Help in Every Need

In every need let me come to You with
   humble trust, saying:
Jesus, help me.
In all my doubts, temptations, and troubles
   of mind,
Jesus, help me.
When I am lonely or tired,
Jesus, help me.
When my plans and hopes have failed,
in all my disappointments and sorrows,
Jesus, help me.

When others let me down,
and Your grace alone can assist me,
Jesus, help me.

When my heart is heavy with failure
and when I see no good come from my ef-
    forts,
Jesus, help me.
When I feel impatient,
and when my cross is hard to carry,
Jesus, help me.
When I am ill,
and my head and hands cannot work,
Jesus, help me.
Always, always,
in spite of weakness and falls of every kind,
Jesus, help me, and never leave me.

Prayer for Zest for living

O Lord,
no matter what may befall me,
let me never lose my zest for life
or my appreciation of this beautiful world
that You have created and made available
    to me.
Keep ever before my eyes the glory of being
    alive,
the wondrous freshness of each new day,
and the magnificence of the creatures
    around us

as they sing Your praises by their very
  being.

Do not let me focus on my own troubles
and remain blind to life's wonders.
Teach me how to take time each day
to thank You for all your gifts to us,
singing Your glory with all Your creatures
in union with Your Son Jesus Christ.

Prayer To Walk with God

Lord God,
the life of today is frantic and delirious.
I often find myself lost in the crowd,
conditioned by whatever surrounds me,
unable to stop and reflect.

Make me rediscover
and live
the value of walking toward You,
laden and compromised
with all the reality
of today's world;
the consciousness of feeling
constantly
called by name, by You;
the grace of responding freely,
of taking Your Word
as light
to all my steps.

Prayer To Discern God's Plan Made Known in Everyday Life

Lord Jesus Christ,
You came to earth and had an immesura-
ble effect
on the lives of those whom You met.
Let me realize that Your Father works
through people I meet every day of my life.
In every encounter and in every event,
You are coming to meet me—
if only I can discern Your presence.
And by my own life I also become for
others
a bearer of God's plan
Help me to respond to Your call gladly
when it comes to me each day in others.

Prayer To Be Truly Human

Lord Jesus Christ,
You came to earth and embraced our hu-
manity,
thereby teaching us how to be truly human.
Help me to follow Your example
and so bring out in myself all that is fully
human.
Teach me to appreciate the immense good
that lies in being human,
climaxed by the gift of genuine self-giving.
Enable me to make use of all Your gifts

in accord with the purpose for which You
   gave them
and for the good of others.
Make me realize that only when I am
   genuinely human
can I be a true follower of You.

Prayer for Love of God

My God and Father,
I believe that You are Love itself.
Give me a deeper love for You.
I believe that You sent Your Son Jesus
to save the world,
and that Your enduring love is always
at work among us.

Help me to keep Your commandments,
for only then do I truly love You.
Give me a love for you that drives out fear,
a love worthy of a child of God.
Through love may I be incorporated into
   Jesus Christ,
Your Son, the true God and eternal Life!

Prayer for Love of Neighbor

Lord Jesus,
You teach me that the greatest of all vir-
   tues is love.
I earnestly ask for an increase
of true love for my neighbor.
Give me a love that is long-suffering,

kind not envious,
not self-seeking, and not irritable.

Let my love take note of injury,
and refuse to rejoice when injustice triumphs
but rather be joyful when truth prevails.
Make it a love that is ready to make allow-
    ance,
that always trusts and hopes,
and is ever patient.
May my love be kind, merciful, and forgiv-
    ing
in imitation of Your Father's love for me.

Prayer To Know and Follow
One's Vocation

Heavenly Father,
You have created us in such a way
that each has some state in life to pursue
for the good of the whole human race
and Your holy Church.
Help me to know my vocation
and to follow it with joy and dedication.
No matter what problem I may encounter,
let me never lose hope,
aware that You have given me the talents
to succeed in any state to which You call
    me.

Prayer of Gratitude for Speech

Lord Jesus Christ,
You said that Your words were spirit and
    life
and Your listeners exclaimed
that no one had ever spoken like You be-
    fore.
I give You thanks for my gift of speech
by which I can praise Your goodness and
    majesty
and communicate with my fellow humans.
Grant that my words may always be such
as to honor You and help others,
and transmit only sentiments leading to
    eternal life.
And if I fail, please be forgiving
and enable me to start anew.

Prayer for a Retreat

Lord Jesus Christ,
You told the Apostles
to retire to a desert place and rest a while.
I am taking this time to follow Your exam-
    ple.
Grant that I may obtain all the fruits
that I can from this retreat.

Enable me to make it in union with You,
to know myself better and to get closer to
    You.

Help me to listen attentively,
to ponder prayerfully,
and to speak wisely.
Let me emerge from this spiritual renewal
as a more committed Christian,
better equipped to advance along the path
that You have laid out for me.

Prayer for One's Name Day

Lord Jesus Christ,
today I celebrate the Saint whose name I
  bear.
It is a special day for me
and should bring me closer to my Patron
as well as to You and the Father.
Inspire me to strive ever harder
to imitate my Patron's virtues on earth
and come to join him/her in heavenly
  glory.

Prayer to a Patron Saint

Dear St. N.,
I have been honored to bear your name—
a name made famous by your heroic virtues.
Help me never to do anything to besmirch
  it.
Obtain God's grace for me
that I may grow in faith, hope, and love,
and all the virtues.

Grant that by imitating you

I may imitate your Lord and Master, Jesus Christ.

Watch over me along the way of the rest of my life

and bring me safe to my heavenly home at my death.

Prayer on One's Birthday

Almighty God,

today is the anniversary of my birth,

the day on which You allowed me to enter

this magnificent world that You have made.

Let me be convinced that my birth meant something,

despite the very ordinariness of my life.

Make me realize that You set me on this earth

for a reason,

and that I must continue to work

to carry out Your plan in every respect.

Thank You for creating me

and for redeeming me.

Teach me the fleetingness of time

and the enduring length of eternity.

Help me to remain close to You until my death,

starting from now,

which is the first day of the rest of my life.

Prayer for Friends

Lord Jesus Christ,
while on earth You had close and devoted
    friends,
such as John, Lazarus, Martha, and Mary.
You showed in this way
that friendship is one of life's greatest
    blessings.

Thank You for the friends that Your have
    given me
to love me in spite of my failures and weak-
    nesses,
and to enrich my life after Your example.
Let me ever behave toward them
as You behaved toward Your friends.
Bind us close together in You
and enable us to help one another on our
    earthly journey.

Prayer for Relatives

Lord of heaven,
You poured out the gifts of charity
into the hearts of Your faithful
by the grace of the Holy Spirit.
Grant health of mind and body
to Your servants for whom we pray.
Make them love You with all their hearts
and practice with perfect love

only those things that are pleasing to You.
Keep them safe from all harm
and bring them all to Your eternal home
after their earthly pilgrimage.

Prayer for Benefactors

Heavenly Lord,
I ask you to pour out Your blessings
on all those who have helped me along
    life's way,
whether I am aware of their contribution or
    not.
Bless those who taught me in living and in
    the Faith,
those who ministered to my spiritual
    needs,
those who worked to make my life easier,
those who befriended me along the way,
those who prayed and sacrificed for me,
and those who gave their lives for my wel-
    fare.
Grant Your blessing to all of them
whether they are living or dead,
and bring them all into the glorious light
of Your eternal Kingdom.

INDEX OF PRAYER THEMES

(Bold type indicates the eight divisions of the book)